The Soul Calendar

and the Lemniscate

The Soul Calendar and the Lemniscate

Essays and a New Translation

by

Barbara Betteridge

Rudolf Steiner College Press

Cover design: Daniel Nordaas and Claude Julien
Cover drawing: Keiko Papic

ISBN 0-945803-69-9

Book orders may be made through
Rudolf Steiner College Bookstore:
Tel. 916-961-8729, Fax. 916-961-3032
Catalog and online orders: www.steinercollege.edu
Questions or comments, E-mail: bookstore@steinercollege.edu

Rudolf Steiner College Press
9200 Fair Oaks Boulevard
Fair Oaks, CA 95628, U.S.A.

Table of Contents

Preface

Barbara Betteridge, born in Santa Barbara, California in 1913 (the year after the Soul Calendar was published), was the daughter of an internationally known ornithologist, who sought lifelong in both science and religion for ultimate answers. It was her mother, however, who "found" Rudolf Steiner in 1927 and sent her husband a copy of *Occult Science*. After reading it he wrote her, "That man knew what he was talking about." And then he died.

Barbara joined the Anthroposophical Society when she was twenty-one. Her lifelong love affair with words, especially with poetry, led her to study literature and languages. Dr. Poppelbaum urged her to translate verse. When she was twenty-eight (just entering the age of the gemuet soul), an editor from Anthroposophic Press asked her to translate the lecture that is now the first in the collection published under the title *The Reappearance of the Christ in the Etheric*. There, in the first paragraph, she met the translation challenge of the word *Gemüt*.

She dedicated her whole life to Anthroposophy: serving as secretary to the Los Angeles Branch of the Anthroposophical Society for many years; translating Rudolf Steiner's lectures and verse; and through free lance writing, especially on the Soul Calendar and on the gemuet.

Barbara died in Fair Oaks, California in 2002, still perfecting her last translation just hours before her passing.

The present volume, published posthumously, is an offering of some of her works. While the verses and To Wonder at Beauty are "finished" in her mind, the other essays have not received her fine tuning.

Thanks are due: to her husband of 67 years, Dick Betteridge, for decades of support and sharing in anthroposophical study and typing the many rewrites; to Dennis Klocek for his interest; to Helen Lubin for encouragement and editing; to Carol Knight for the final typing; and to Keiko Papic for the cover art work.

Jonitha Hasse
Hillsdale, New York, 2004

To Wonder at Beauty

A robin's ethereal matin announces the dawn from high in a pine. The daisy and I turn our faces to greet the rising Sun. The cat yawns, stretches, and begins to look for breakfast. One of us "knows" that the Sun is a physical object in space, and that it is an awesome number of miles away. To the astronauts who must depend on computations to rendezvous their tiny craft with a distant object, such mileage matters. They need Copernican astronomy.

But when the Sun rises in majesty over the mountains, my soul and I do not need a computer to tell us how long ago its light left the Sun. No more does the daisy, just opening her eye. No more does the robin. We worship in our different ways, keeping the time of day, the time of year.

Once in the house again, I give myself to questions; I wonder and I ponder. I think of a poet of long ago who wrote of "rosy-fingered dawn" in another language. Why do events like sunrises, solstices, and spring move men so? —The daisy (day's eye) opens because she must. I doubt the robin decides whether to sing today or to sulk. The cat is moved only by his own importances. We alone, who are Man, have a choice whether to worship or to ignore.

A memory rises. I see myself as a child, camping out on the Mojave Desert late on a moonless night. The obtrusive glare of civilization had not yet found it, nor had the obtrusive roar of a thousand cars. Even our one car had been a rarity on the desert that day. With no air conditioner—no windows for that matter—it had been hot. My father was tired from the strain of keeping the car in a pair of sandy ruts, challenging enough to the teams we met pulling wagons. After a supper my mother had cooked on a campfire, we had stood together in awe before the splendor of a desert sunset, had shared a bedtime prayer, and settled into our blankets spread on the sand.

Now, in the darkness, with the campfire out and voices stilled, the very intensity of the silence began to suggest to a sensitive child an awesome Presence hovering over all. I still remember the awe that filled me, looking up at the firmament of stars—thousands of stars—crowding so close overhead. I remember the moment my breath caught as one of them blazed silently across the sky. How does a child feel who sees "Beauty bare"?

It was not a vacation trip. My father was an ornithologist and writer who did his own photography in the day of heavy cameras, glass slides and no telephoto lenses. We were on our way to the Sierras, pulling a trailer loaded with photographic and climbing gear. Once there, my mother would busy herself with cooking and camp chores while my father would study and photograph the birds, make scientific notes, and, when moved, write too, with the seeing eyes and hearing heart of a poet. (Long after his death, an anthroposophist, reading a few pages of his voluminous *Birds of California* would point out to me that he had been a Goethean scientist. I knew only that he had been greatly esteemed, indeed that he had been included, along with Thoreau, Audubon, John Muir, and Joseph Wood Krutch in a book entitled *American Naturists*. Were these not Goethean scientists?)

The next day we wound our way up to the Mammoth Lakes area to our final campsite. Here, my primary task after helping my mother gather firewood was, as usual, to be neither seen nor heard. I was almost forced to spend my time looking and listening. So I breathed in what was around me and bit my lip in silence.

The majesty of the High Sierras remains today. Nothing can change that. But few children today are exposed to the pristine beauty that reigned then, when the air was crystalline and the silences were enhanced rather than broken by the soft sounds of the wind through undisturbed forest, by gently lapping waters and lilting birdsongs. The lilting bird names echo in my memory, as my father would report seeing a lazuli bunting, a pine siskin, or a pair of pileated woodpeckers or my favorite, the one named after him, which nested among glaciers: *leucosticte tephrocotis dawsoni*. I would repeat its name softly, like a refrain.

I don't remember at what point I came to consider Nature as my best friend. When we were at home I had no playmates, and by the strange circumstances of my karma I was as lonely during the school years as during summer in the mountains. I had had the misfortune to be, at the age of two, what is now called a spontaneous reader. Age six had found me in fourth grade, age eight in sixth, a solemn little girl in pigtails and a homemade dress, always set apart from the other girls who came to school in limousines from a different world. When Teacher was present students ignored me. When she was absent I was teased and tormented.

In time, the heroes of literature came to my rescue. I met Robin Hood in a reader and at once became Robin. Free days would find me riding out from Sherwood Forest on my fiery steed surrounded by my "merry men," ready for deeds of derring-do on behalf of those who needed them. What the neighbors saw was a rather scraggly little girl rolling an old tire down the country road, but I was in a New World, and it was mine. There were other times, still, when I sat dreaming on the broad limb of an old oak, listening to the hum of Nature and watching her small events around me.

When I was thirteen, Destiny took my mother and me to Ohio to join my father, who had been there for a year. My parents were busy. I was alone as usual. But there was a beautiful park across from our house—beautiful until October. The trees lost their lovely green leaves! —Nature was dead! It might as well have been God who was dead. The child of everlasting summer in California, now I was really alone.

That winter I found the human world. I made friends and "worshiped" human models. When spring came to the park, its never-before-experienced beauty was ecstasy. It began to stir the poetic in my soul. But I could enjoy it—and leave it. As an adult I would be grateful to Destiny for this awakening and its timing.

There is one more chapter which belongs to the story. After a year, Mother and I returned to our home in Santa Barbara. My father had to stay in Ohio. But he and I became close at last through letters and shared poems. One day in late May when I was fifteen, I was sitting under the old favorite oak, dreamily musing, when a mood of heightened awareness came over me. Everything in nature around me—the mockingbird singing, the hummingbird that whirred close, the roses in the garden, the ferns, the very leaves—seemed to be speaking to me of God. I wrote a poem which began:

> The dreamy summer days have come again,
> Pervading solitary garden nooks
> With drowsiness sublime...

My father never saw that poem. The next day, class was interrupted by a message for me. My father had died unexpectedly. At once I knew, "That is why that experience came to me yesterday in the garden. God knew this had to happen and was preparing me to understand." Nature, my old friend, had been the messenger.

"They" would go on trying to teach me that the universe is only a vast ocean of gases and fragments of whirling rock (or something of the sort) and that I am only a speck of sand, as it were, tossed up for a moment on an uncaring beach. Fortunately, this fable impressed me only briefly. It didn't really ring my bell.

I had been indoctrinated by too many sunsets, too many birdsongs, too many mountain peaks and desert nights, and yes, by poetry and prayer, and by admirable human beings, both real and fictive. In retrospect, I had been a fortunate child. Now, I turned to my father's library, full of science, philosophy, religion, and more recently metaphysics—everything a lifelong seeking could turn to for answers. But I was not bookish. I read only two or three of his volumes. One gave me what I needed. Years later I learned that it was plagiarized Steiner. But it was enough. It would carry me through the darkness of college until I had time to seek more books and the people to match them, time to take up my own questions.

It would be many years and many chapters later that I would come to realize that the capacity "to wonder at beauty" and to "look up to the noble" —elusive as the breath that bears it, belongs to an element of soul which Rudolf Steiner had named "the human Gemüt."

The human Gemüt is at once the organ of the poet's art and of the Goethean scientist. This *gemuet* is not identical with the heart, I would come to realize, but dwells beside the heart in the human breast, forming by way of perceptive feeling a kind of bridge between the brain with its intellectual thinking and the heart as organ of higher consciousness and moral will. Heart and gemuet together, then, may be seen to be essential not only in reuniting Man with the divine sources of his origin, but in supporting him in his appointed tasks as a co-creator in "world-becoming."

Rudolf Steiner's Soul Calendar, which begins with what we call the Easter Mood, Osterstimmung in German, suggests one path. (It is helpful to note that this title in German means "Easter tuning" —tuning of the gemuet, as the German dictionary gives it. The secondary meaning, "mood," is then the result). The words resound:

> When out of the wide World-horizon
> The Suns speaks to man's perceiving
> And joy from very deeps of soul
> Unites with the Light in our beholding,
> Then stream from out the Selfhood's sheath
> Our thoughts into Space's distances
> And subtly bond
> Man's Being with the being-life of Spirit.

The Living Year
The Story of the Soul Calendar

> *Observing the course of the year means: accompanying the great Cosmic Artist and letting those things which Heaven impresses upon the Earth become living again in one's self in might images, which, however, become realities for the human gemuet.*
>
> Rudolf Steiner
> "The Christmas Imagination"

Some years ago, a story found its way to my mailbox in a clipping from *The London Observer* telling of a Sufi mystic who had long carried the question, "What is the mystical path of the Christian?" It finally dawned on him that it is a meditative path through the seasons of the year, marked by the Christian festivals.

Then the mystic found himself asking a further question: "Who might the gurus of the Christians be?" In due course it dawned on him: They all share the same guru! They call him Christ.

Who among the Christians who read this rather astonishing piece would have found sense in it, unless it might be one who thought of Rudolf Steiner's little volume *The Calendar of the Soul* with its festival moods marking the seasons? To be sure, such a reader would not have called the Calendar's a mystical path. In anthroposophical terms he might have thought of it, rather, as a path by which the human *I*, active in the consciousness soul, can interrelate with the cosmos through its developed feeling nature, or gemuet soul. For it was this gemuet which Rudolf Steiner had later spoken of as being capable of entering into a living relationship with the whole cosmos once it really comes to life. (September 27, 1923)

Over the years countless thousands have followed the beckoning of the Calendar's path, many of them forced to depend on the guideposts of translations which can never do justice to the consummate artistry of the original verses. —Even so, many have surely experienced intimations, dawnings, Eureka events. It was such an event for me when a friend in Germany wrote me that she had heard a lecturer who related the Soul Calendar to the lemniscate. She knew of the unrest I was feeling because the teacher of a course I was taking on the Soul Calendar related the year only to the circle. —Isn't going 'round and 'round unchangingly like being tied to the wheel concept of life that is characteristic of ancient India, I wondered? —How can a free spirit resonate to such a concept, such an image? But a lemniscate, hence a lemniscatory path through the year? This would be dynamic! This would be living! Was it not the perfect image?

Of course! In my mind's eye I could already see it as the perfect image of Earth's and Man's inward/outward breathing relationship to the Cosmos during the course of the year. Later I would see with caught breath the beautiful drawing of the lemniscate Rudolf Steiner had made without comment on Easter Eve of 1923, which appears in *The Cycle of the Year as Breathing Process of the Earth*. The diagram shown here, in which I tried to delineate the Soul Calendar relationships, was first printed in an article in the Dornach Newsletter in 1969.

Rudolf Steiner described the Soul Calendar (in 1912) as offering "a path leading from the human soul to the living Spirit weaving through the Universe." Scientist Guenther Wachsmuth called the Calendar succinctly "an instrument of spiritual striving." Some have found it to be a path of initiation. H.D. van Goudoever and Walther Bühler, for example, have described such paths. Many others have found it to awaken creative impulses in their gemuets—impulses to draw or paint or fashion their own poetic responses to the unfolding revelations of the year.

If the Calendar is indeed a reality, as countless thousands have experienced it, it is obvious that individual meditants everywhere will have had, continue to have, many shared Eureka moments.

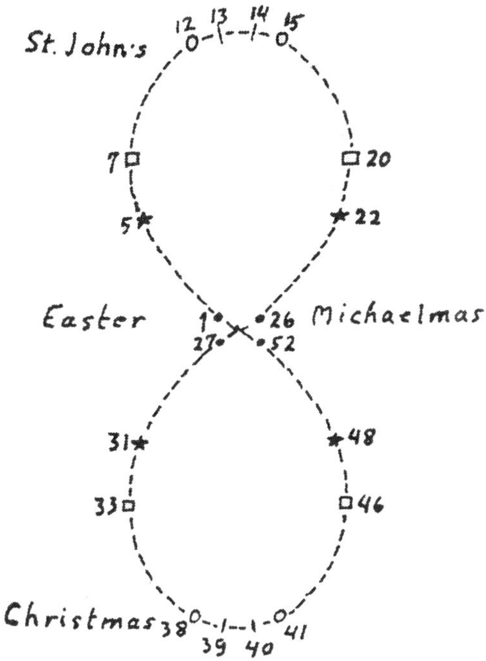

II

One may be the realization that superimposed on the lemniscate stands the traditional Christian Cross, its arms reaching toward Easter and Michaelmas, just above the crossing point. This verifies the cosmic horizon pictured in the Easter verse—experiences which together with Michaelmas form a balance between the summer experience of the Mysteries of the Heights (top of lemniscate) and the winter experience of the Mysteries of the Depths (at the bottom).

Yet it is probable that few today know even that the Soul Calendar verses themselves originally filled only the last 20 pages of a 92-page volume, all of which was fraught with significance—a significance still not fully recognized. At the time of its appearance in the spring of 1912, the volume was often met with, in Rudolf Steiner's words, "mockery and derision."

First, there was the mystifying cover, pictured here, whose message translates: *In the Year 1879 after the Birth of the "I."* There was no title otherwise. Nor was there an author. Rudolf Steiner's name did not appear on or in the little volume.

The preface, also challenging, was entitled simply: What is Intended. It introduced a weekly Star Calendar with "intuitive" drawings—Rudolf Steiner's word—which had been made under his guidance by Imma von Eckhardstein. These drawings were strange and puzzling to those who saw them. Steiner explained that these new zodiacal signs are an expression of what souls need to learn in this epoch. They were meant to indicate, not physical constellations, as the usual signs for the zodiac have come to do, but rather the spiritual forces, the beings active in the cosmos.

The moon phases, and also a listing of historical dates of births, deaths and other events over centuries, painstakingly researched by Dr. Steiner, appeared under these drawings week by week. Only after all this did the reader find the section entitled "Soul Calendar,"with its own preface, followed by the 52 meditative verses, beginning with the verse "Easter Mood."

Consternation abounded among those around Rudolf Steiner. —How would he explain the book's strange cover? Since he had not yet found the right time to "announce" the ascendancy of the Archangel Michael associated with 1879, he explained the date by saying only that it had been that many years since the event of Golgotha in the year 33. The cover design was meant to proclaim that event as marking the birth of the *I*, of the ego-consciousness, in every human being, regardless of race, nationality or religion. Easter of the year 33, Rudolf Steiner asserted, rather than the Jesus Child's birth, was the appropriate date with which to begin a calendar year of universal significance.

Can we not imagine the outcry? Why, such a calendar would mean that years would be of unequal length! Resignedly, Rudolf Steiner responded that indeed the world at large could not be expected to take up such an impulse, but that it would be important for the members of the Anthroposophical Society to observe an Easter to Easter year among themselves. In a lecture devoted to the Soul Calendar [Cologne May 7, 1912], he explained: "In what is unequal there is life; in what is uniform and fixed there is the impress of death. Our Calendar is intended to be a creative impulse for life." Once again, we find implications without end.

> I myself regard the second part, the Calendar of the Soul, as very important, [Rudolf Steiner continued in this lecture:] I can assure you that the results of long, long occult investigations are contained in these 52 verses which will enable the soul to find access to happenings in the great universe and thereby to experience the Spirits working in the onward flow of time. . . .
>
> These meditation formulae are not easy to make one's own. For this the human soul will need many years. It is not a sudden idea that is documented in this Calendar, [he is referring to the whole Calendar] but rather a deed which stands in organic connection with our whole movement.

Do we not sense a more than usual urgency in Rudolf Steiner's defense of this new impulse, this *deed*, as though he feared it might fall by the wayside unrecognized? —It was that same Easter, that same cosmic hour, which had seen an impulse that we recognize to be an essential part of the Anthroposophical movement's task of establishing the New Mysteries in the fifth epoch. We speak of the lecture cycle then called *Reincarnation and*

Karma and Their Significance in Modern Culture. —This we know fell largely on unhearing ears.

Surely it says something for the strength not only of the spiritual yearnings dwelling below the surface in the twentieth century, but of the reality of what Rudolf Steiner would describe later as worldwide hosts of human beings dedicated to the furtherance of what we have come to know in Anthroposophy as Michael culture. These human beings—we ourselves—are inwardly motivated to seek to develop such a world culture, and in so doing to recognize every human being as a free individual. Since then thousands of individuals who use the Soul Calendar verses in their diverse languages recognize themselves as being part of the movement. —But in 1912 it was still impossible to mention the Archangel Michael and his hosts, or his connection with the year 1879.

If we ask ourselves at century's turning how the Calendar impulse has fared, it is clear at least that the impulse is carried today in the hearts of many, many a meditant of the Soul Calendar. We may be aware, too, that the Calendar has also inspired quietly working individuals in small groups to carry on the impulse of the Star Calendar, notably those whom we think of as astrosophers, beginning with Elisabeth Vreede and including above all Willi Sucher. Some of these individuals have through this work also developed deeper insights into the mysteries of reincarnation.

An eminent theologian who recognized the significance of the Calendar impulse at mid-century should still be mentioned. Emil Bock devoted a lecture to exploring the significance of Rudolf Steiner's mantric verse, from 1906 on. He described the Soul Calendar as no less than "the fulcrum, in a certain way, in the whole of Rudolf Steiner's life work." Indeed he reported that when Rudolf Steiner was once asked in what way the soul could most effectively prepare itself to experience the Etheric Christ, he had answered: "Through the meditative experience of the year's course. The mysteries of the seasons are Nature's gift for the meditating human being who seeks the Christ sphere." (*Newsletter of the Anthroposophical Society in America,* Winter 1981–82).

In the medieval Paradise Play, so beloved in Waldorf schools around the world, when Gabriel chases Adam and Eve out of the garden, he promises to recall them "late and slow." Many today are beginning to realize that if we are ever to regain a conscious connection with the god or gods of our beginning, it will have to be out of our own free will, our own endeavor. The Soul Calendar offers a path.

The Lemniscate in Your Life

You are not likely to find a lemniscate in your garden on a summer's day—or on any other—unless, like a friend of mine, you chance to be watching a small granddaughter running about, see her begin to weave two trees together with an invisible figure eight. In pure delight she repeats the sequence over and over, savoring the primal joy it gives her, so a grandmother told me.

Geometricians have noted numerous lemniscate forms, but it is the so-called Bernoulli lemniscate which we know as a figure eight. This exists as a two-dimensional object in the visible world only when someone draws it, perhaps with a pen, perhaps with ice skates. In the invisible world, however, it may gradually dawn on us that it has a significant role to play as a divine creative principle.

The word *lemniscate* is said to have originated from the story of a Greek marathon runner, who after a race, threw down his headband, or *lemma,* and became entranced with the 8-form in which it lay on the ground. Inside had become outside, outside inside. Many of us know the specialness of experiencing the lemniscate in movement, in ice skating or in eurythmy.

Another aspect that belongs to its reality is the essential part the lemniscate plays in the life of plants. For we may find that in the garden the lemniscate shows itself to be an invisible principle. For every plant, already when it opens its seed-coat to step into the world, harbors the crossing-point of a lemniscate. This is the point from which one shoot emerges upward-bound toward the Sun, and another downward-bound into the Earth. Physically, it is described as a layer that may be only one cell wide. —Yet we may also, in our mind's eye, begin to see both an upper and a lower loop of invisible beings and forces who are concerned from then on—that is, in the realm of time—with the plant's life and growth.

This crossing-point image of the plant seems to be as near as the lemniscate comes to existing physically in the realm of Nature. For in essence, the lemniscate lives in movement, in rhythmic movement. It can be the movement of a child running around two trees, of a skater on the ice, of a eurythmist following the form, or even of a conductor's arm or our own arm.

We may be reminded also of that ancient symbol, the Caduceus, the staff carried by Mercury, formed of two snakes winding together. Our imagination brings up the image of the Mercury pillar carved in wood in the First Goetheanum and now represented in plaster.

The life of the plant through the seasons also reflects the changing picture of the relation of Sun and Earth through the year, a relation that may be seen to embody—almost but not quite visibly—the lemniscate.

In man, too, we find the lemniscate, especially in the principle, the image, underlying the breathing process. We have the capacity as human beings to develop such a mental image (*Vorstellung*) and through it to open up new realms to our own cognition.

I can tell you of a personal path opened up to my husband and me by the lemniscate. My husband, of a scientific bent, set out somehow to prove visibly the alleged lemniscatory relationship of Sun and Earth. The opportunity came the first time he retired. We had moved to a rural community in Southern California where Dick could take advantage of the floor of our sunny patio to record the story. He molded a ball of wax to a size that, suspended from a beam, would cast a distinct shadow on the concrete floor. Then he recorded with a small dot of white paint the position of the shadow, day after sunny day at the exact second of noon. Over time certain observations became apparent. First, that as the Sun approached the equinoxes the spaces between the dots widened; as the Sun approached the solstices the spaces narrowed, the dots even overlapping each other. One noticed also that at the summer solstice the shadow fell close to the ball of wax; in winter, far out. After several months the form of the lemniscate became predictable.

As I pondered the result, it came to me that every statue and every tree is recording an invisible lemniscate. That must be what the ancient Egyptians were up to, then, as they erected the obelisks in the middle of a sun-drenched landscape!

Thoughts on Translation
True Poetry and the Soul Calendar

As the King James translation of Genesis tells us, the Spirit of God *moved* upon the face of the waters before He said, "Let there be Light." Although the plurality of the creating Gods has been translated out (It is *Elohim* in Hebrew, *Exusiai* in esoteric christology, *Spirits of Form* in occult science), the centrality of Light to all creation is clear. We might also note that the principle of movement as a primary force already glimmers here. If we picture to ourselves Michelangelo's painting of God creating Adam, isn't power-filled movement the very essence of the figure of God?

It becomes less strange, then, when we read that Rudolf Steiner said that every true poem—which is also the product of creative activity—is formed out of eurythmic gesture. This was already known, he said, in those mystery centers in which forms of eurythmic gesture were practiced long ago. (July 10, 1924)

Most readers will be aware that eurythmy is an art of movement which Rudolf Steiner drew from spiritual sources, and which, like other *true* arts, can form a bridge for us to these sources. The two kinds of eurythmy reveal in gesture the movements inherent in music and in poetry. Every sound, musical or spoken, is experienced subliminally by the human being as an impulse to movement, even if we suppress this movement. For the human body came from the same source and was formed according to the same laws as music and the spoken word. A *true* poem creates in all reality a bridge to the source. A translation can offer only a stronger or a weaker rope, cast hopefully across the abyss.

As an example of a true poem, Rudolf Steiner once cited Goethe's lines

> Über allen Gipfeln
> Ist Ruh'.

These five words offer a good example of the untranslatable. The sense is: Over the mountaintops (or hilltops) is rest. However you see it or say it, it is clear that what makes the original "true poetry" eludes translation. —What are the problems?

We will find, if we explore it, that *Ruh'* or *Ruhe* has many dimensions. Rudolf Steiner once said it had "magical power." —Say it slowly. The power of a word cannot be separated from its sound, its eurythmic gesture. One can experience the quality of this word in the meditation Rudolf Steiner gave, beginning "I bear *Ruhe* within me." —The English word which most directly translates it, *rest*, however, is almost an opposite eurythmically. It ends in a plosive sound—*T*, which is anything but restful. In *Knowledge of the Higher Worlds*, it is easy to sense why the translator chose *inner tranquility* instead of *inner rest* to translate *innere Ruhe*. Other near synonyms are peace, ease, calm, quietude, repose—and refreshment. But none of these has the confluence of sound and meaning that we find in *Ruhe*.

In the Matthew Gospel we read that Jesus Christ promised rest to those who were "heavy laden," as Jehovah before Him had often promised His people rest. I am told that the Greek word used in the Matthew Gospel, αναπαυσις, suggests the refreshment that comes from rest. The word occurs twice in the passage, and both times is translated *rest* in English. But Martin Luther translated it once *Ruhe* and the second time "quickening" (*Erquickung*), thus suggesting both connotations.

We begin to see the risks in doing or in relying on translation. —Even at its best, it loses force in two directions: in both gesture and meaning.

Anyone who can recite (experiencing the movement) even a few lines of the poetry of Homer, Shakespeare, Goethe or Rudolf Steiner in their original languages will recognize their ineffable magic, will recognize that even though a translation may also be stirring, it will not ring the same bells. —Imagine trying, yourself, to translate Blake's "Tiger, tiger burning bright" into another language, or even to say it differently in English. This poem rises more than most out of the realm of meaning, accessible to the intellect, to speak almost exclusively to the gemuet-soul, which experiences those qualities

that can be known only through perceptive feeling.
The first line of the first verse of the Soul Calendar, which is clearly true poetry already through its sounds, can deliver only its meaning in translation—can speak only to the intellect—and that somewhat lamely. —Here we have loss of the gesture.

In verse seven, Rudolf Steiner says that now in late May our thinking's power inclines to lose itself in the senses' *Schein*. —The senses' show? The senses' glory? the translator asks herself. —It could be either one—or both. The reader of German makes the call out of himself, according to his own perceptive feeling, his own insight. The student using a translation must draw his illumination through a darkened glass.

Dr. Karl König in one of his essays on the Soul Calendar marveled at the way every word is just the right word in just the right place. —It rests there, we might suggest, waiting for its cue, for its time in the course of the year to speak to the questing human gemuet, to the seeking heart, to be spoken by the human voice and given back to the cosmos and its divinities by way of the human breath, in a delicate intercourse.

When we know the gemuet to be the soul element through which we engage in art, and especially poetry, know, too, that the process is dependent physiologically on our breathing system, it comes as a pleasant surprise to find signs of this awareness surfacing in today's culture. America's recent poet laureate, Robert Hass, observed not long ago: "Art occurs when you put the structure of breathing into other people's bodies." He went on to say:

> There's a sense in which poetry is not so much the writing of words as it is the movement of breath itself. To write it, you must pay attention to the breathing of poetry, to all speech as breath. . . . *Spiritus* was breath in Latin. When you think about it, breath may be the way to feel yourself into the constant exchange that our lives involve, giving away the air and taking it back, and giving it away and taking it back until we see that even our ideas and feelings are just a giving and taking back. . . . When one says somebody else's poem aloud, one speaks in *that* person's breath.

Although it might seem to be a by-path from the subject, we should not leave hanging in mid-air Steiner's statement that Ruhe has magical power. For this purpose, to call it "rest" will suffice. Indeed, as rest, we find it associated with that force with which we began our observations—that of movement.

In the remarkable *Gospel According to Thomas* which surfaced only in 1945 in a tomb in Upper Egypt, we find a significant saying, which we will quote in the context in which it occurs:

> Jesus said: "If two make peace with each other in this one house, they shall say to the mountain: 'Be moved,' and it shall be moved. . . ."
>
> Jesus said: "If they say to you: 'From where have you originated?' say to them: 'We have come from the Light, where the Light has originated through itself.' . . ."
>
> If they ask you: 'What is the sign of your Father in you?' say to them: 'It is a movement and a rest.'"

This, then, is the ultimate source of the created world: A movement and a rest. We find this reality reflected by the genius of the German language, which calls the planets the *moving stars* and what we call the fixed stars *stars of rest*. It is their ever-changing relationships which we experience as the forces of time, to which the Soul Calendar would bring us closer.

If we go back to a lecture Rudolf Steiner gave on eurythmy in 1924, we note that he had found the same principle in the enduring sources open to the seer:

> Let us imagine that the Gods, out of their divine primeval activity, were to make those eurythmic movements which correspond to the sounds of the alphabet. Then, if these movements were impressed into physical matter, the human being would stand before us. This is what really lies behind eurythmy. The human being as we

> see him is a completed form. But the form has been created out of movement. . . . Movement does not proceed from quiescence (*Ruhe*). On the contrary, that which is in a state of rest originates in movement. . . . God eurythmetizes, and as a result of his eurythmy there arises the form of man.
>
> from *Eurythmy as Visible Speech*

Although Rudolf Steiner was speaking of the creation of man here, we have seen from Genesis that the same principle applied to the creation of the cosmos, with which we are seeking a more conscious union, a re-linking, in meditating the Soul Calendar verses.

Rudolf Steiner said at the time it appeared that the Soul Calendar is meant "so to work in the soul that the soul can find the connection between its own inner experience and that which is directed by divine-spiritual beings in the flow of time." (May 7, 1912)

We will see that the language these primal forces speak out of the cosmic "periphery" to the "center" of individual man—what we experience in the course of the year's time—is expressed in the changing nuances of light and in the "festival moods" that arise in our souls as we participate in the cosmic drama of the year.

Is not the Soul Calendar a response to the cry of John the Baptist: The Light shone in the darkness and the darkness comprehended it not? —To the extent that the darkness of the translator must inevitably dim the light of that which would as true art help dispel the darkness—let the translator of the verses printed here urge you to learn to read them in the original language, which you will also find included here.

The Soul Calendar

Verses

in the original German
and in English

The dates given for each verse are those for 1912 and 1913 when Rudolf Steiner gave this series. He stressed the importance of beginning with the first verse at Easter, regardless of when Easter falls in any particular year. Then follows the set interval from Easter until Ascension and Whitsun. The spacing of the following verses, up until St. John's, can be adjusted to accommodate the number of intervening weeks. From there on the weekly intervals are regular, given the fixed dates for St. John's, Michaelmas, and Christmas. The spacing of the verses after Christmas can again be adjusted to accommodate the variable span of time until Easter.

Frühling

A. Oster-Stimmung
(7.–13. April)

1. Wenn aus den Weltenweiten
Die Sonne spricht zum Menschensinn
Und Freude aus den Seelentiefen
Dem Licht sich eint im Schauen,
Dann ziehen aus der Selbstheit Hülle
Gedanken in die Raumesfernen
Und binden dumpf
Des Menschen Wesen an des Geistes Sein.

Z. Michaeli-Stimmung
(29. September)

26. Natur, dein mütterliches Sein,
Ich trage es in meinem Willenswesen;
Und meines Willens Feuermacht,
Sie stählet meines Geistes Triebe,
Dass sie gebären Selbstgefühl,
Zu tragen mich in mir.

Herbst

Ā. Siebenundzwanzigste Woche
(6.–12. Oktober)

27. In meines Wesens Tiefen dringen:
Erregt ein ahnungsvolles Sehnen,
Dass ich mich selbstbetrachtend finde,
Als Sommersonnengabe, die als Keim
In Herbstesstimmung wärmend lebt
Als meiner Seele Kräftetrieb.

Z̄. Zweiundfünfzigste Woche
(30. März)

52. Wenn aus den Seelentiefen
Der Geist sich wendet zu dem Weltensein
Und Schönheit quillt aus Raumesweiten,
Dann zieht aus Himmelsfernen
Des Lebens Kraft in Menschenleiber
Und einet, machtvoll wirkend,
Des Geistes Wesen mit dem Menschensein.

Spring

A. Easter Mood
(7–13 April)

1. When out of the wide World-horizon
The Sun speaks to man's perceiving
And joy from very deeps of soul
Unites with the Light in our beholding,
Then stream from out the Selfhood's sheath
Our thoughts into Space's distances
And subtly bond
Man's Being with the being-life of Spirit.

Z. Michaelmas Mood
(29 September)

26. O Nature, thy maternal essence
I bear within the Being of my will,
And fiery power of my will,
This steels my spirit's impulses
That they may bring to birth Self-feeling
To bear myself in me.

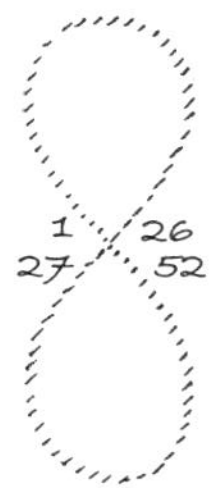

Autumn

Ā. Twenty-seventh Week
(6–12 October)

27. To delve into my Being's depths
Awakens longing filled with dawning vision,
That self-observing I may find myself
As gift of Summer's Sun, which as a seed
Lives warmingly in Auturmn's mood
As germinating forces of my soul.

Z̄ Fifty-second Week
(30 March)

52. When out of the deeps of soul
The Spirit turns to the Cosmic life of being
And Beauty wells from widths of Space,
Then out of Heaven's distances there streams
The force of Life into human bodies
And working mightily unites
The Spirit's Being with the being-life of Man.

B. Zweite Woche
(14.–20. April)

2. Ins Äussre des Sinnesalls
Verliert Gedankenmacht ihr Eigensein;
Es finden Geisteswelten
Den Menschensprossen wieder,
Der seinen Keim in ihnen,
Doch seine Seelenfrucht
In sich muss finden.

Y. Fünfundzwanzigste Woche
(22.–28. September)

25. Ich darf nun mir gehören
Und leuchtend breiten Innenlicht
In Raumes- und in Zeitenfinsternis.
Zum Schlafe drängt natürlich Wesen,
Der Seele Tiefen sollen wachen
Und wachend tragen Sonnengluten
In kalte Winterfluten.

B. Achtundzwanzigste Woche
(13.–19. Oktober)

28. Ich kann im Innern neu belebt
Erfühlen eignen Wesens Weiten
Und krafterfüllt Gedankenstrahlen
Aus Seelensonnenmacht
Den Lebensträtseln lösend spenden,
Erfüllung manchem Wunsche leihen,
Dem Hoffnung schon die Schwingen lähmte.

Y. Frühling-Erwartung
(23.–29. März)

51. Ins Innre des Menschenwesens
Ergiesst der Sinne Reichtum sich,
Es findet sich der Weltengeist
Im Spiegelbild des Menschenauges,
Das seine Kraft aus ihm
Sich neu erschaffen muss.

B. Second Week
(14–20 April)

2. Into the outer world of sense
The power of Thought its separate being loses;
The Spirit worlds are finding
Again their human offspring,
Who needs to find his seed in them,
And yet his fruit of soul
Must find within himself.

Y. Twenty-fifth Week
(22–28 September)

25. Now may I to myself belong
And shining spread an inner light
Into the dark of Space and Time.
Toward sleep all natural being presses;
Yet deeps of soul should now awaken
And waking carry Sun's warm glowing
Into chilly Winter's flowing.

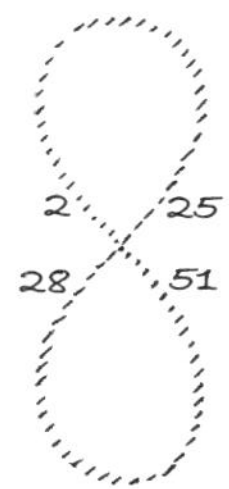

B̄. Twenty-eighth Week
(13–19 October)

28. I can now inwardly enlivened
Feel my own Being's wide horizons
And filled with strength, shed rays of thought
From out the soul's Sun-power,
To help resolve life's riddles,
And grant fulfillment to many a wish
Whose wings had long been lamed by hope.

Ȳ. Expectation of Spring
(23–29 March)

51. Into the inner Being of Man
The riches of the senses pour;
The Spirit of the World now finds Himself
In the mirror of the human eye,
Which out of Him its power
Must now create anew.

C. Dritte Woche
(21.–27. April)

3. Es spricht zum Weltenall,
Sich selbst vergessend
Und seines Urstands eingedenk,
Des Menschen wachsend Ich:
In dir, befreiend mich
Aus meiner Eigenheiten Fessel,
Ergründe ich mein echtes Wesen.

X. Vierundzwanzigste Woche
(15.–21. September)

24. Sich selbst erschaffend stets,
Wird Seelensein sich selbst gewahr;
Der Weltengeist, er strebet fort
In Selbsterkenntnis neu belebt
Und schafft aus Seelenfinsternis
Des Selbstsinns Willensfrucht.

C̄. Neunundzwanzigste Woche
(20.–26. Oktober)

29. Sich selbst des Denkens Leuchten
Im Innern kraftvoll zu entfachen,
Erlebtes sinnvoll deutend
Aus Weltengeistes Kräftequell,
Ist mir nun Sommererbe,
Ist Herbstesruhe und auch Winterhoffnung.

X̄. Fünfzigste Woche
(16.–22. März)

50. Es spricht zum Menschen-Ich,
Sich machtvoll offenbarend
Und seines Wesens Kräfte lösend,
Des Weltendaseins Werdelust:
In dich mein Leben tragend
Aus seinem Zauberbanne,
Erreiche ich mein wahres Ziel.

C. Third Week
(21–27 April)

3. There speaks unto the Cosmic All,
Itself forgetting
And mindful of its primal state
The waxing 'I' of Man:
"In Thee, if I can free myself
From fetters of my own devising
I find the ground of my true being."

X. Twenty-fourth Week
(15–21 September)

24. Itself creating steadily
Soul-being of itself becomes aware.
The Cosmic Spirit is striving on,
In self-cognition newly livened,
Creating from soul-darkness
The sense-of-selfhood's fruit of will.

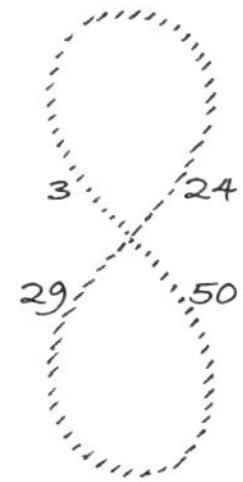

C̄. Twenty-ninth Week
(20–26 October)

29. Oneself the light of thinking
To kindle forcefully within,
Interpreting experience
From Cosmic Spirit's well of forces:
This is my Summer's heritage,
My source of Fall's repose and Winter's hope.

X̄. Fiftieth Week
(16–22 March)

50. There speaks unto the 'I' of Man,
Itself with might revealing
And setting free its Being's forces,
The World-existence's joy-in-becoming:
"Into thee my life transporting
From out of its enchanted bond
I reach my own true goal."

D. Vierte Woche
(28. April–4. Mai)

4. Ich fühle Wesen meines Wesens:
So spricht Empfindung,
Die in der sonnerhellten Welt
Mit Lichtesfluten sich vereint;
Sie will dem Denken
Zur Klarheit Wärme schenken
Und Mensch und Welt
In Einheit fest verbinden.

$\overline{\text{D}}$. Dreissigste Woche
(27. Oktober–2. November)

30. Es spriessen mir im Seelensonnenlicht
Des Denkens reife Früchte,
In Selbstbewusstseins Sicherheit
Verwandelt alles Fühlen sich.
Empfinden kann ich freudevoll
Des Herbstes Geisterwachen:
Der Winter wird in mir
Den Seelensommer wecken.

W. Dreiundzwanzigste Woche
(8.–14. September)

23. Es dämpfet herbstlich sich
Der Sinne Reizesstreben;
In Lichtesoffenbarung mischen
Der Nebel dumpfe Schleier sich.
Ich selber schau in Raumesweiten
Des Herbstes Winterschlaf.
Der Sommer hat an mich
Sich selber hingegeben.

$\overline{\text{W}}$. Neunundvierzigste Woche
(9.–15. März)

49. Ich fühle Kraft des Weltenseins:
So spricht Gedankenklarheit,
Gedenkend eignen Geistes Wachsen
In finstern Weltennächten,
Und neigt dem nahen Weltentage
Des Innern Hoffnungsstrahlen.

D. Fourth Week
(28 April–4 May)

4. "I feel the very essence of my Being."
So speaks perceptive feeling,
Which in the Sun-illumined world
Unites itself with floods of Light.
It would on thinking
Bestow its warmth for clarity
And Man and World
In oneness firmly bind.

W. Twenty-third Week
(8–14 September)

23. Now dims autumnally
The senses' effort to entice;
With revelations of the Light
Dull veils of mist commingle.
And I behold in widths of Space
The Autumn's winter sleep.
Lo, Summer has to me
Herself now given over.

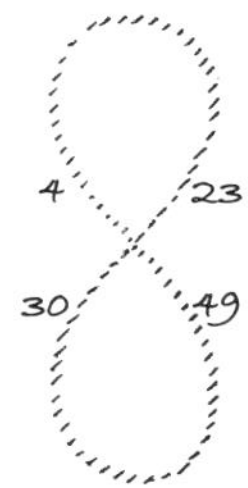

D̄. Thirtieth Week
(27 October–2 November)

30. There sprout in sunlight of my soul
The ripened fruits of thinking;
To self-awareness' certainty
All feeling now transforms itself.
And filled with joy I can perceive
The Autumn's spirit-wakening:
Lo, Winter will awake in me
The Summer of the soul.

W̄. Forty-ninth Week
(9–15 March)

49. "I feel the power of Cosmic being-life";
So speaks my clarity of thought,
Rememb'ring its own spirit's growth
In dark of cosmic-nights,
And bending on World-day's approach
Its inner being's rays of hope.

E. Fünfte Woche
(5.–11. Mai)

5. Im Lichte, das aus Geistestiefen
Im Raume fruchtbar webend
Der Götter Schaffen offenbart:
In ihm erscheint der Seele Wesen
Geweitet zu dem Weltensein
Und auferstanden
Aus enger Selbstheit Innenmacht.

V. Zweiundzwanzigste Woche
(1.–7. September)

22. Das Licht aus Weltenweiten,
Im Innern lebt es kräftig fort:
Es wird zum Seelenlichte
Und leuchtet in die Geistestiefen,
Um Früchte zu entbinden,
Die Menschenselbst aus Weltenselbst
Im Zeitenlaufe reifen lassen.

Ē. Einunddreissigste Woche
(3.–9. November)

31. Das Licht aus Geistestiefen,
Nach aussen strebt es sonnenhaft:
Es wird zur Lebenswillenskraft
Und leuchtet in der Sinne Dumpfheit,
Um Kräfte zu entbinden,
Die Schaffensmächte aus Seelentrieben
Im Menschenwerke reifen lassen.

V̄. Achtundvierzigste Woche
(2.–8. März)

48. Im Lichte, das aus Weltenhöhen
Der Seele machtvoll fliessen will,
Erscheine, lösend Seelenrätsel,
Des Weltendenkens Sicherheit,
Versammelnd seiner Strahlen Macht,
Im Menschenherzen Liebe weckend.

E. Fifth Week
(5–11 May)

5. Within the Light that out of Spirit's deeps
Is weaving fruitfully in Space
The Gods' creation manifests:
In this appears the Soul's own Being
To cosmic life and being widened
And risen now
From narrow selfhood's inner sway.

V. Twenty-second Week
(1-7 September)

22. The Light from out the world-horizons
Lives on in me with power;
Becoming light of soul
It shines into the spirit's deeps
To liberate the fruits
Which let the human self from Cosmic Self
In Time's long cycles ripen.

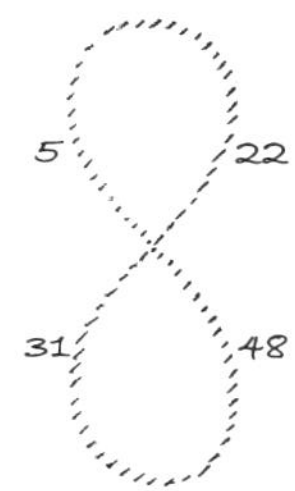

Ē. Thirty-first Week
(3–9 November)

31. The Light from out the Spirit's deeps
Is striving outward like a Sun;
Becoming life's own force of will,
It shines into the senses' dullness,
To liberate the forces
Which let creative powers ripen
From soul incentives in the work of Man.

V̄. Forty-eighth Week
(2–8 March)

48. Within the Light that out of Cosmic heights
Would stream into my soul with power,
May there shine forth unraveling soul riddles,
The Cosmic thinking's certitude,
And rallying its rays' full might
Awaking love within the human heart.

F. Sechste Woche
(12.–18. Mai)

6. Es ist erstanden aus der Eigenheit
Mein Selbst und findet sich
Als Weltenoffenbarung
In Zeit- und Raumeskräften;
Die Welt, sie zeigt mir überall
Als göttlich Urbild
Des eignen Abbilds Wahrheit.

U. Einundzwanzigste Woche
(25.–31. August)

21. Ich fühle fruchtend fremde Macht
Sich stärkend mir mich selbst verleihn,
Den Keim empfind ich reifend
Und Ahnung lichtvoll weben
Im Innern an der Selbstheit Macht.

F̄. Zweiunddreissigste Woche
(10.–16. November)

32. Ich fühle fruchtend eigne Kraft
Sich stärkend mich der Welt verleihn;
Mein Eigenwesen fühl ich kraftend
Zur Klarheit sich zu wenden
Im Lebensschicksalsweben.

Ū. Siebenundvierzigste Woche
(23. Februar–1. März)

47. Es will erstehen aus dem Weltenschosse,
Den Sinnenschein erquickend, Werdelust.
Sie finde meines Denkens Kraft
Gerüstet durch die Gotteskräfte,
Die kräftig mir im Innern leben.

F. Sixth Week
(12–18 May)

6. There has arisen from its separate state
My Self to find itself
As cosmic revelation
Within the forces of Time and Space;
The World shows everywhere to me
As godly archetype
The truth of my own image.

U. Twenty-first Week
(25–31 August)

21. I feel a foreign power fruiting
And growing stronger lend myself to me.
I feel the life-seed ripening
And dawning vision light-filled weave
Within me on the Selfhood's power.

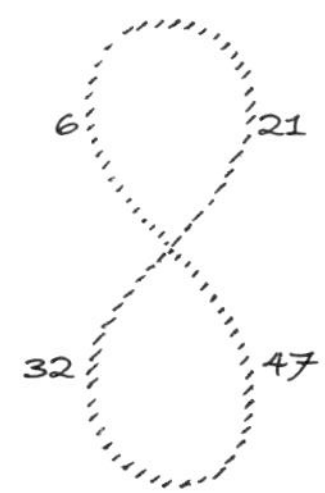

$\overline{\text{F}}$. Thirty-second Week
(10–16 November)

32. I feel a force my own fruit-bearing
And growing stronger grant me to the world;
I feel my very Being growing
In strength to turn toward clarity
In weaving of life's destiny.

$\overline{\text{U}}$. Forty-seventh Week
(23 February–1 March)

47. There wills to arise from out the cosmic womb,
Requickening the senses' show, joy in becoming.
May it find my thinking's power
Well armed by very powers of God
Which powerfully in me dwell.

G. Siebente Woche
(19.–25. Mai)

7. Mein Selbst, es drohet zu entfliehen,
Vom Weltenlichte mächtig angezogen.
Nun trete du mein Ahnen
In deine Rechte kräftig ein,
Ersetze mir des Denkens Macht,
Das in der Sinne Schein
Sich selbst verlieren will.

T. Zwanzigste Woche
(18.–24. August)

20. So fühl ich erst mein Sein,
Das fern vom Welten-Dasein
In sich sich selbst erlöschen
Und bauend nur auf eignem Grunde
In sich sich selbst ertöten müsste.

$\bar{G}$. Dreiunddreissigste Woche
(17.–23. November)

33. So fühl ich erst die Welt,
Die aussser meiner Seele Miterleben
An sich nur frostig leeres Leben
Und ohne Macht sich offenbarend,
In Seelen sich von neuem schaffend,
In sich den Tod nur finden könnte.

$\bar{T}$. Sechsundvierzigste Woche
(16.–22. Februar)

46. Die Welt, sie drohet zu betäuben
Der Seele eingebor'ne Kraft;
Nun trete du, Erinnerung,
Aus Geistestiefen leuchtend auf
Und stärke mir das Schauen,
Das nur durch Willenskräfte
Sich selbst erhalten kann.

G. Seventh Week
(19–25 May)

7. My Self is threatening to flee away,
By cosmic Light too powerfully drawn.
Now enter thou, my dawning vision,
And firmly claim thy rights.
Replace in me the thinking's power
Which in the senses' show
Inclines to lose itself.

T. Twentieth Week
(18–24 August)

20. Now only do I feel my very being
Which far from the World's existence
Would in itself itself extinguish,
And building only on its own foundation
Would in itself bring death upon itself.

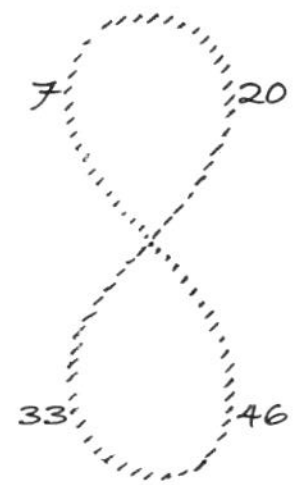

$\bar{\text{G}}$. Thirty-third Week
(17–23 November)

33. So now I feel the World
Which left without my soul's participation
Reveals but frozen empty life,
Devoid of power of its own,
Renewing itself in human souls,
While in itself it could find but death.

$\bar{\text{T}}$. Forty-sixth Week
(16–22 February)

46. The World is threatening to benumb
My Soul's own inborn force.
Now enter thou, my Memory,
From deeps of Spirit shining forth
And strengthen my beholding
Which only through the force of will
Is able to uphold itself.

H. Achte Woche
(26. Mai–1. Juni)

8. Es wächst der Sinne Macht
Im Bunde mit der Götter Schaffen,
Sie drückt des Denkens Kraft
Zur Traumes Dumpfheit mir herab.
Wenn göttlich Wesen
Sich meiner Seele einen will,
Muss menschlich Denken
Im Traumessein sich still bescheiden.

H̄. Vierunddreissigste Woche
(24.–30. November)

34. Geheimnisvoll das Alt-Bewahrte
Mit neuerstandnem Eigensein
Im Innern sich belebend fühlen:
Es soll erweckend Weltenkräfte
In meines Lebens Aussenwerk ergiessen
Und werdend mich ins Dasein prägen.

S. Neunzehnte Woche
(11.–17. August)

19. Geheimnisvoll das Neu-Empfang'ne
Mit der Erinn'rung zu umschliessen,
Sei meines Strebens weitrer Sinn:
Er soll erstarkend Eigenkräfte
In meinem Innern wecken
Und werdend mich mir selber geben.

S̄. Fünfundvierzigste Woche
(9.–15. Februar)

45. Es festigt sich Gedankenmacht
Im Bunde mit der Geistgeburt,
Sie hellt der Sinne dumpfe Reize
Zur vollen Klarheit auf.
Wenn Seelenfülle
Sich mit dem Weltenwerden einen will,
Muss Sinnesoffenbarung
Des Denkens Licht empfangen.

H. Eighth Week
(26 May–1 June)

8. The senses' might is growing
In union with the Gods' creating,
Subduing thinking's power
To dullness of a dream in me.
If now a godly Being
Would with my soul unite,
Then human thinking must
In dream existence humbly bide.

S. Nineteenth Week
(11–17 August)

19. Now hiddenly that which is new conceived
Within my memory to ensheathe—
This be my striving's further aim:
And growing strong it shall awaken
My own forces in my inner being
And in becoming give myself to me.

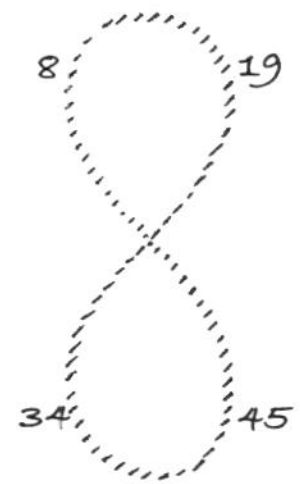

H̄. Thirty-fourth Week
(24–30 November)

34. Now hiddenly what was preserved of old
To feel within me quickening
With new-arisen being of its own:
May this, in waking me,
Pour cosmic forces into my life's outer work
And in becoming imprint me in existence.

S̄. Forty-fifth Week
(9–15 February)

45. The power of thought is growing firm
In union with the Spirit-birth;
It lights dim stirrings of the senses
Into fuller clarity.
If soul's abundance
Would unite with the World's becoming,
Then senses' revelation
Must receive the light of thinking.

I. Neunte Woche
(2.–8. Juni)

9. Vergessend meine Willenseigenheit
Erfüllet Weltenwärme sommerkündend
Mir Geist und Seelenwesen;
Im Licht mich zu verlieren
Gebietet mir das Geistesschauen,
Und kraftvoll kündet Ahnung mir:
Verliere dich, um dich zu finden.

R. Achtzehnte Woche
(4.–10. August)

18. Kann ich die Seele weiten,
Dass sie sich selbst verbindet
Empfangnem Welten-Keimesworte?
Ich ahne, dass ich Kraft muss finden,
Die Seele würdig zu gestalten,
Zum Geistes-Kleide sich zu bilden.

$\overline{I}$. Fünfunddreissigste Woche
(1.–7. Dezember)

35. Kann ich das Sein erkennen,
Dass es sich wiederfindet
Im Seelenschaffensdrange?
Ich fühle, dass mir Macht verlieh'n,
Das eigne Selbst dem Weltenselbst
Als Glied bescheiden einzuleben.

$\overline{R}$. Vierundvierzigste Woche
(2.–8. Februar)

44. Ergreifend neue Sinnesreize
Erfüllet Seelenklarheit,
Eingedenk vollzogner Geistgeburt,
Verwirrend sprossend Weltenwerden
Mit meines Denkens Schöpferwillen.

I. Ninth Week
(2–8 June)

9. When I forget my own quite separate will,
The cosmic warmth announcing summer fills
My spirit and soul-being.
In light to lose myself
My spirit's seeing bids me now,
And dawning vision strongly tells me:
"Lose thou thyself to find thyself."

R. Eighteenth Week
(4–10 August)

18. Can I make wide my soul
That she unite herself
With Cosmic seed-Word new conceived?
It dawns on me that I must find the power
To fashion worthily my soul
That she may form a garment for the Spirit.

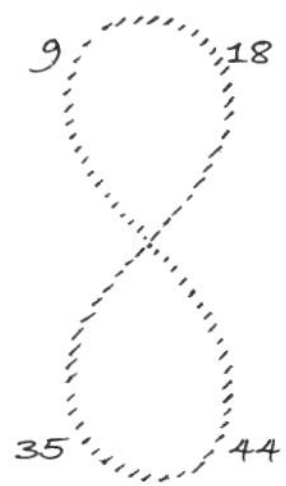

Ī. Thirty-fifth Week
(1–7 December)

35. Can I so know what it is "to be"
That beingness may be found anew
In my soul's creative urge?
I feel that power is lent to me
Which humbly lets this self of mine
Indwell the Cosmic Self as member.

R̄. Forty-fourth Week
(2–8 February)

44. In grasping senses' new enticements
My clarity of soul,
Now mindful of the Spirit-birth achieved,
Fills wildering sprouting World-becoming
With my own thinking's creator-will.

J. Zehnte Woche
(9.–15. Juni)

10. Zu sommerlichen Höhen
Erhebt der Sonne leuchtend Wesen sich;
Es nimmt mein menschlich Fühlen
In seine Raumesweiten mit.
Erahnend regt im Innern sich
Empfindung, dumpf mir kündend,
Erkennen wirst du einst:
Dich fühlte jetzt ein Gotteswesen.

Q. Siebzehnte Woche
(28. Juli–3. August)

17. Es spricht das Weltenwort,
Das ich durch Sinnestore
In Seelengründe durfte führen:
Erfülle deine Geistestiefen
Mit meinen Weltenweiten,
Zu finden einstens mich in dir.

$\bar{\text{J}}$. Sechsunddreissigste Woche
(8.–14. Dezember)

36. In meines Wesens Tiefen spricht
Zur Offenbarung drängend
Geheimnisvoll das Weltenwort:
Erfülle deiner Arbeit Ziele
Mit meinem Geisteslichte,
Zu opfern dich durch mich.

$\bar{\text{Q}}$. Dreiundvierzigste Woche
(26. Januar–1. Februar)

43. In winterlichen Tiefen
Erwarmt des Geistes wahres Sein;
Es gibt dem Weltenscheine
Durch Herzenskräfte Daseinsmächte;
Der Weltenkälte trotzt erstarkend
Das Seelenfeuer im Menscheninnern.

J. Tenth Week
(9–15 June)

10. To lofty heights of summer
The radiant Being of the Sun ascends:
He takes along my human feeling
Into His own wide realms of Space.
In dawning vision, stirs within
Perceptive feeling, softly telling me:
"One day thou'lt come to know
A godly Being touched thee now."

Q. Seventeenth Week
(28 July–3 August)

17. There speaks the Cosmic Word
Which I through senses' portal
Could lead into my soul's own ground:
"Fill thou thy spirit's deeps
With My wide world-horizons
To find at last Myself in thee."

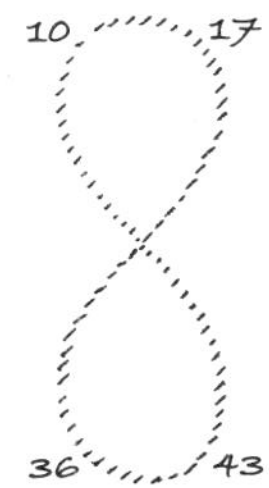

J̄. Thirty-sixth Week
(8–14 December)

36. There speaks within my Being's depths
Toward revelation pressing,
Yet hiddenly the Cosmic Word:
"Fill thou the aims of all thy work
With Spirit Light of Mine
To offer up thyself through Me."

Q̄. Forty-third Week
(26 January–1 February)

43. Within the wintry deeps
True being-life of Spirit warms;
It gives to world appearance
Through heart's own forces the power to be;
Soul's fire within Man's inner Being
In growing strong defies World-Cold.

K. Elfte Woche
(16.–23. Juni)

11. Es ist in dieser Sonnenstunde
An dir, die weise Kunde zu erkennen:
An Weltenschönheit hingegeben,
In dir dich fühlend zu durchleben:
Verlieren kann das Menschen-Ich
Und finden sich im Welten-Ich.

P. Sechzehnte Woche
(21.–27. Juli)

16. Zu bergen Geisteschenk im Innern,
Gebietet strenge mir mein Ahnen,
Dass reifend Gottesgaben
In Seelengründen fruchtend
Der Selbstheit Früchte bringen.

Winter

K̄. Siebenunddreissigste Woche
(15.–21. Dezember)

37. Zu tragen Geisteslicht in Weltenwinternacht
Erstrebet selig meines Herzens Trieb,
Dass leuchtend Seelenkeime
In Weltengründen wurzeln,
Und Gotteswort im Sinnesdunkel
Verklärend alles Sein durchtönt.

P̄. Zweiundvierzigste Woche
(19.–25. Januar)

42. Es ist in diesem Winterdunkel
Die Offenbarung eigner Kraft
Der Seele starker Trieb,
In Finsternisse sie zu lenken
Und ahnend vorzufühlen,
Durch Herzenswärme, Sinnesoffenbarung.

K. Eleventh Week
(16–23 June)

11. It is for thee in this Sun-hour
To recognize the tidings wisdom-filled:
To beauty of the world surrendered,
Yet feeling thyself in thee, discover:
The human I can lose itself
And find itself in the Cosmic I.

P. Sixteenth Week
(21–27 July)

16. To shelter Spirit gift within
My dawning vision sternly bids me,
That ripening, gifts of God
In soul's deep ground grown fertile
May bring their fruits to selfhood.

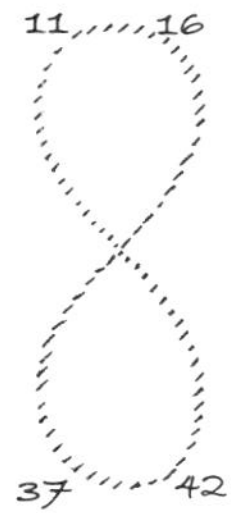

Winter

K̄. Thirty-seventh Week
(15–21 December)

37. To bear the Light of Spirit
into world's winter night
My heart's impulse is striving in its bliss,
That, shining, seeds of soul
May root in World foundations
And God's Word sound in senses' darkness
Transfiguring, through all that Is.

P̄. Forty-second Week
(19–25 January)

42. It is within this winter-gloom
The manifesting of a power her own
Which is the soul's strong impulse,
To guide herself into realms of darkness,
In dawning vision there to feel
Through warmth of heart the senses' revelation.

L. Johannes-Stimmung
(24. Juni)

12. Der Welten Schönheitsglanz,
Er zwinget mich aus Seelentiefen
Des Eigenlebens Götterkräfte
Zum Weltenfluge zu entbinden;
Mich selber zu verlassen,
Vertrauend nur mich suchend
In Weltenlicht und Weltenwärme.

O. Fünfzehnte Woche
(14.–20. Juli)

15. Ich fühle wie verzaubert
Im Weltenschein des Geistes Weben.
Es hat in Sinnesdumpfheit
Gehüllt mein Eigenwesen,
Zu schenken mir die Kraft,
Die, ohnmächtig sich selbst zu geben,
Mein Ich in seinen Schranken ist.

$\bar{L}$. Weihe-Nacht-Stimmung
(22.–28. Dezember)

38. Ich fühle wie entzaubert
Das Geisteskind im Seelenschoss;
Es hat in Herzenshelligkeit
Gezeugt das heil'ge Weltenwort
Der Hoffnung Himmelsfrucht,
Die jubelnd wächst in Weltenfernen
Aus meines Wesens Gottesgrund.

$\bar{O}$. Einundvierzigste Woche
(12.–18. Januar)

41. Der Seele Schaffensmacht,
Sie strebet aus dem Herzensgrunde,
Im Menschenleben Götterkräfte
Zu rechtem Wirken zu entflammen,
Sich selber zu gestalten
In Menschenliebe und im Menschenwerke.

L. St. John's Mood
(24 June)

12. The shining beauty of the world
Impels me out of deeps of soul
In my own life the powers of Gods
To free for cosmic flight,
Myself now to forsake
And trustingly to seek myself
In Cosmic Light and Cosmic Warmth.

O. Fifteenth Week
(14–20 July)

15. I feel as though bound into spell
In the world's bright show, the spirit's weaving.
It has in sense's dullness
Enshrouded my own Being,
To give to me the strength
Which caught within its narrow bounds
My 'I' is powerless to give itself.

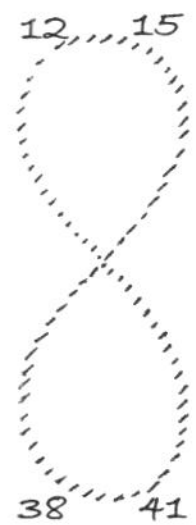

L̄. Christ-mass Mood
(22–28 December)

38. I feel as if from spell unbound
The Spirit's Child in womb of soul;
Within my heart's own brightness
Has holy Word of Worlds begotten
High heaven's fruit of hope
That jubilant grows to world's far reaches
From out my Being's ground in God.

Ō. Forty-first Week
(12–18 January)

41. The soul's creative might
Is striving from the heart's deep ground
To kindle to right action
In human life the powers of Gods,
And thus to shape and mold herself
In human love and human working.

M. Dreizehnte Woche
(30. Juni–6. Juli)

13. Und bin ich in den Sinneshöhen,
So flammt in meinen Seelentiefen
Aus Geistes Feuerwelten
Der Götter Wahrheitswort:
In Geistesgründen suche ahnend
Dich geistverwandt zu finden.

N. Vierzehnte Woche
(7.–13. Juli)

14. An Sinnesoffenbarung hingegeben
Verlor ich Eigenwesens Trieb,
Gedankentraum, er schien
Betäubend mir das Selbst zu rauben,
Doch weckend nahet schon
Im Sinnenschein mir Weltendenken.

M̄. Neununddreissigste Woche
(29. Dezember–4. Januar)

39. An Geistesoffenbarung hingegeben
Gewinne ich des Weltenwesens Licht.
Gedankenkraft, sie wächst
Sich klärend mir mich selbst zu geben,
Und weckend löst sich mir
Aus Denkermacht das Selbstgefühl.

N̄. Vierzigste Woche
(5.–11. Januar)

40. Und bin ich in den Geistestiefen,
Erfüllt in meinen Seelengründen
Aus Herzens Liebewelten
Der Eigenheiten leerer Wahn
Sich mit des Weltenwortes Feuerkraft.

M. Thirteenth Week
(30 June–6 July)

13. And when I am in senses' heights
There flames within my deeps of soul
From fire-worlds of Spirit
The Gods' own Word of Truth:
"With dawning vision seek in Spirit grounds
To find thyself akin to Spirit."

N. Fourteenth Week
(7–13 July)

14. To senses' revelation given over
I lost the drive of my own Being,
And thought-dream, dazing me,
Did seem to rob me of myself.
Yet waking me draws near
In senses' glory Cosmic Thinking.

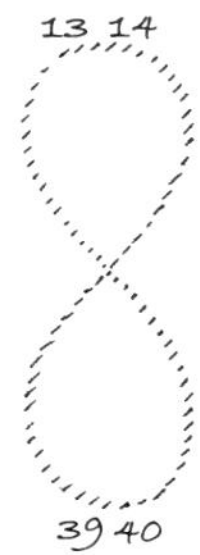

M̄. Thirty-ninth Week
(29 December–4 January)

39. To Spirit's revelation given over
I win the Cosmic Being's Light.
My thinking's power waxes;
Becoming clear, it gives itself to me,
And waking me, it frees in me
Through thinker's might my feeling of Self.

N̄. Fortieth Week
(5–11 January)

40. And when I am in Spirit's deeps,
Then in my soul foundations,
From out the heart's own realm of Love
My separate nature's vain illusion
Is filled with fire-force of Cosmic Word.

Bibliography

In references to works by Rudolf Steiner, the GA number is the volume in the bibliographic survey of his complete works in German.

Betteridge, Barbara. "1969—The Recurrence of the Soul Calendar Year," *Goetheanum Newsheet* 1969.

Bock, Emil. "The Creation of Mantric Verse in the Course of Rudolf Steiner's Life," *Anthroposophical Society in America Newsletter*, Winter 1981–1982.

Buhler, Walther. *Das bewegliche Osterfest.* Tubingen, Germany: Katzmann-Verlag, 1965.

Dawson, William Leon. *The Birds of California.* San Diego: South Moulton Co, 1923.

The Gospel According to Thomas. New York: Harper, 1959.

Goudoever, H.D. van. *A Contemplation about Rudolf Steiner's Calendar of the Soul*. Spring Valley, NY: St. George Publications, 1984.

Hass, Robert, in Bill Moyers, *The Language of Life*. New York: Doubleday, 1995.

König, Karl. *Rudolf Steiner's Calendar of the Soul: A Commentary.* London: Rudolf Steiner Press, 1977.

Krutch, Joseph Wood. *American Naturists*. New York: E.P. Dutton, 1930.

"The Paradise Play." *Christmas Plays from Oberufer*, Bristol: Rudolf Steiner Press, 1993.

Steiner, Rudolf. "Anthroposophy and the Human Gemüt," lecture given September 27, 1923 in Vienna; published in *Michaelmas and the Soul-Forces of Man*. Spring Valley, NY: Anthroposophic Press, 1946. GA 223.

_______. "Calendar of the Soul." Cologne, 7 May 1912. Translation by D. S. Osmond published in *Anthroposophical Quarterly*, Vol. 8, No. 1, 1963, pp 90–95. GA 143.

_______. "The Christmas Imagination," lecture given October 26, 1923 in Dornach, Switzerland. Published in *The Four Seasons and the Archangels*. London: Rudolf Steiner Press, 1968. GA 229.

_______. *The Cycle of the Year as Breathing Process of the Earth*, lectures given March 31–April 8, 1923 in Dornach Switzerland. Translated by Barbara Betteridge and Frances E. Dawson. Spring Valley, NY: Anthroposophic Press, 1984. GA 279.

_______. *Eurythmy as Visible Speech*. London: Anthroposophical Publishing Company, 1956. GA 279.

_______. *Knowledge of the Higher Worlds*, also published as *How to Know Higher Worlds*. Hudson, NY: Anthroposophic Press, 1994. GA 10.

_______. *Man and the World of Stars: The Spiritual Communion of Mankind*, lectures given November 26–December 31, 1922 in Dornach, Switzerland. New York: Anthroposophic Press, 1963. GA 219.

_______. *Occult Science*, also published as *An Outline of Esoteric Science*. Hudson, NY: Anthroposophic Press, 1997.

_______. *Reappearance of Christ in the Etheric*. Spring Valley, NY: Anthroposophic Press, 1983.

_______. *Reincarnation and Karma and their Significance in Modern Culture*, lectures given January–March 1912 in Berlin and Stuttgart. Steiner Book Centre, 151 Carisbrook Crescent, N. Vancouver V7N 2S2, Canada, 1977.

_______. *Wahrspruchworte*. Dornach: Rudolf Steiner Verlag, 1978. This book contains the weekly verses of the Soul Calendar, the version from which Barbara Betteridge drew her text.

_______. *Supersensible Knowledge: Anthroposophy as a Demand of the Age*. Hudson, NY: Anthroposophic Press, 1987. GA 84.

Wachsmuth, Guenther. *The Life and Work of Rudolf Steiner*. New York: Whittier Books, Inc, 1955.

Barara Betteridge left us a rich legacy of essays, mostly on the subject of the *Gemüt*. Some were published in anthroposophical journals, some she did not herself clear for publication. They may be purchased for the cost of copying and postage from:

Rudolf Steiner Library
65 Fern Hill Rd
Ghent, NY 12075